# THE PRAYERS OF BLACK AND BROWN MOTHERS

COMPILED BY DR. BARBARA WHITEHEAD

# TABLE OF CONTENTS

# INTRODUCTION

Black and Brown mothers are crying out to God who undoubtedly hears and answers prayers. It is an intense time of difficulty, trouble, and pain. Crisis demands attention, and actions must be taken to address these unstable, uncertain, unjust, and often unpredictable situations. The perils of our time are not the results of random, isolated, unexpected activities. It results from years of

human subjugation, hidden plans, secret forces, health and financial disparities, fears, and

insecurities, vicious mindsets, abuse of power, racism, and absolute hatred.

There is a demand and clamor for change being led by weeping, wailing, mourning mothers. It is an unseen protest: it is a powerful movement of mothers marching, chanting, and crying out for their children to a just God who will not turn them away. Poverty, violence, oppression, and murder have wrapped themselves like a python around the hearts of Black and Brown mothers around the world. The incessant and continued squeeze of injustice has caused them to cry out from the unbearable pain. There is a sound filling the atmosphere and rising to heaven. The land is polluted with the blood of Black and Brown victims.

The blood is crying out to the all-knowing God who hears and sees. Mothers are crying and will not be comforted because their children are being intimidated, abused, captured, and imprisoned. Many are no longer alive. "Hear a just cause, O Lord!" A revival of prayer is arising all over the world. This sound has been heard before. Jeremiah, the Prophet, heard it in his day. It was the sound of bitter weeping and deep anguish. It was the sound of mothers crying out for their

children. They could not remain silent. There was no comfort. Jeremiah said, "A cry was heard in Ramah" (Jeremiah 31:15). Deep anguish and bitter weeping have overtaken the land.

Mother Rachel is weeping for her children. She refuses to be comforted, for her children are gone. Jeremiah heard a prophetic sound. It was the sound produced by devastation designed to subdue a whole nation of people. It was the sound of inconsolable grief.

The most ruthless of tactics used by enemy forces is to kill the children to break the will

of those who are under attack. Jeremiah heard the cries of mothers who watched the massacre of

their children. It was the sound of crisis; it was the sound of an oppressed people being abused

by power and authority that had no regard for the sanctity of their lives. It was a tragedy of unfathomable proportion. Broken hearts, broken families, and broken lives produce a sound.

Black and brown mothers are incessantly crying out as they see their children being killed, captured, and taken into slavery. The prayers of Black and Brown mothers will not be denied; they will not be silenced. God does hear a mother's cry!

This anthology of prayers from the hearts of Black and Brown mothers is a unique compilation of co-authors who represent varying ages and perspectives. Each author shares in a brief biographical format the process of life that led them to the targeted prayer of their heart for this project. Although each author's life plan has been different, there is a common focus that unites.

It is the shared experience of being a Black or Brown mother with the same fears and concerns for the welfare of their children. They share a unique experience because they are black and brown. These mothers have hopes and dreams for the futures of their children. These are mothers who will not give up and have united to seek the resources of heaven by faith and prayer.

These are mothers who embrace the uniqueness of their experiences and celebrate the power of unity as black and brown mothers praying for divine intervention.

You will be enlightened and empowered as you take this journey with black and brown mothers expressing their heartfelt concerns through prayer. We know that a mother's love is universal.

The color of one's skin does not define the authenticity of motherhood. All mothers want what is best for their own. The focus on prayers of Black and Brown mothers is not to negate the concerns of all mothers, but rather it is the empowerment of embracing a unique experience.

Black and Brown mothers must give voice to the unique concerns they experience. All mothers do not have the same concerns. When Jochebed, Moses' mother, was in distress trying to hide her baby from a system that sought to kill him in his infancy, the Egyptian mothers did not have

the same concerns. They were both mothers, true enough, but their experiences in life were

different. The law to kill all the Hebrew baby boys did not apply to the Egyptian baby boys. The

prayers of the Hebrew mothers were consequently different from the prayers of the Egyptian

mothers. (Exodus 2:3) We are honored to give voice to the prayers of Black and Brown mothers.

# CHAPTER 1

*Brenda J. Darling*

*"God is in the midst of her; she shall not be moved; God will help her when the morning dawns." (Psalm 46:5 AMP).*

## Praying for Single Mothers

Brenda J. Darling is a lifelong resident of Florida.

Brenda spent her entire professional career

operating out of her gift and lifelong dream of

being a nurse of 31 years. She has traveled

internationally on medical mission trips to Benin,

West Africa, and the Pampanga District of the Philippines. She's been licensed as an outreach minister through the Embassies of God International Ministry and has served as a prayer

minister for the Morris Cerullo World Prayer Communication Center. She is also certified

as a trained Intercessor through Rise-Up United One Intercessor Ministry.

Brenda is also an Ordained Deaconess in her local church and the Founder of the Women's support group, Grace to Be. Brenda is the proud mother of two adult sons. In her personal time, she enjoys volunteering in the community for various causes, participating in a monthly book club, does home gardening, and spends as much time as possible with her five grandchildren.

\*\*\*\*\*\*\*\*\*\*\*\*\*\*\*\*\*\*\*\*\*\*\*\*\*\*\*\*\*\*\*\*\*\*\*\*\*\*\*\*

I knew the exact moment I had to leave. I know some women must plan when and how they will leave their husbands. They must save enough money to secure housing for themselves and their children. For me, I did not have the luxury of time. I had to escape. The moment I felt the smooth, cold steel of the gun in my hand, I knew I needed to flee. And I had to do it quickly and strategically. This came after the night I determined it was the final beating I would ever take at the hands of my abuser.

My children would never see my dignity dissolve in a slap again or once more be threatened for their lives. I decided the only way to stop it was to stop him. To me, to stop him was to put a bullet through his head. As I held the gun in my hands, I looked at my children lying innocently beside him. If I did this, it would rob them of both parents. Did I have the heart to take away the two people that were the dearest in their young lives? They did not deserve a future without their parents. This was not their fight; it was not their cross to bear. I could not bear to think about what would happen to them. There had to be another way. So, for the moment, I did what I always did.

Let him think all was good; nothing had changed, and he was forgiven. But the moment he left the next morning, so did we. We grabbed all we could salvage, packed it in the car, and left. No note, no goodbye. The kids thought we were going on an unplanned trip, and what a trip it was. I had no money and no real plan. I was 400 miles away from my home, and my home was where I needed to get to. I went to say goodbye to my mother-in-law, who gave me $50. I will always be grateful to her. She told me to take the money and go home, saying, "I'd rather you go now than I have to send you in a box." After seeing my face, she knew what the situation was. Frightened, alone with two kids in tow, I started out on a journey as a single mother headed into homelessness, welfare, and having to rely on God to help me navigate an unexpected life and unknown path. I was stubborn and determined. We moved to his hometown, Miami, with the intention that I would attend Nurse Anesthetist school, but Hurricane Andrew hit within a month of us moving there, and we lost everything. But I was holding on to my plan. We stayed in a motel the first night, but that exhausted the $50. I had worked for a Nursing Agency for daily pay. I did a half-day while my mother-in-law hid the kids. Made enough for a storage unit to put our things in and sheltered us for a few nights.

A lady at work let us crash at her place at night while she worked the night shift, and we had to be out by the time she came home the next morning. I realized this was not going to work when my oldest said he wanted to go to his grandma's house, meaning my mom, and honestly, so did I.

I rented a U-Haul truck, packed up the storage unit, and we were out of Miami for good. And on to the next chapter of our lives.

### Prayer for Single Mothers

*Dear Heavenly Father, I come I humbly come before your throne of grace and into Your divine presence, thanking You for the precious gift of Your Son Jesus and the privilege and opportunity of prayer. What an awesome time to be able to worship and reverence Your Holy Name, for You are Worthy to be praised. Lord, as my mind goes back to when I was a single mother, I recall the struggle, the heartache, the feeling of unworthiness that I would never realize my dreams. But God, as I look at my life now, I know it was only because of You that I am where I am today. Father there are single mothers all over the land who find themselves facing a situation of premeditated calamities in their lives, I ask as they walk through the valleys of the shadows of the demise of relationships in their lives, that you will be with them. Allow them to rest in the shadow of the Highest. Remind them that You will never leave nor forsake them. The men in their lives may have turned their backs, but You, God, will always be there. Let them know, Father, that they have not been forsaken even though they feel lonely and alone, but that your word in Isaiah 41:10 reminds them to fear not and to be not dismayed. Father when they feel down and left out, you will lift them up with Your mighty right hand. We know that when hearts have been shattered many times, you are the glue that puts them back together. You are close to the brokenhearted. When times are hard and provisions are low, remind them that You are their Shepherd, you will provide for all their needs and their children's needs. When shelter is needed, You, oh God, are their shelter even when the raging storms are battering them on every side. If physical shelter is needed, you are a shelter in the time of storm. You are Jehovah Jireh, the Provider of all their needs; spiritual, physical, financial, and emotional. Let these single mothers know as they struggle to raise their children in the admonition of the Lord, nothing they have been through has been wasted. Let them know You, O God, have seen their tears as they cried out to You in the midnight hour, wondering how they were going to make it through another day; dreading how they were going to answer another question about where their father is, or how they were going to stretch another meal when the pantry was getting low. Psalm 62:5-8 says, "My soul, wait thou upon God; for my expectation is from him. He is my rock and my salvation; he is my defense; I shall not be moved. In God is my salvation and my glory; the rock of my strength, and my refuge is in God". Trust in Him always, pour out your heart before him; God you are a refuge for single mothers. I thank you that single mothers can release the concerns of their lives and children to you. Father, I pray that single mothers will stop struggling with the issues of life and release their*

*homes, jobs, anxieties, fears, doubts, and lack over to Jesus today. I pray that they will lay it at your feet and declare it covered under the blood. I bind the enemy in the lives of these single mothers and families and rebuke him from having any part of them in any way, form, or fashion.*

*I declare a God-given spirit of love, unity, peace, guidance, obedience, spiritual devotion, health, and wealth. Father, please go forth in these families and undergird these Queens and single mothers. In Jesus' Name, we pray, amen.*

# CHAPTER 2

*Minister Janice Sales*

*"The Lord is close to the brokenhearted and saves those who are crushed in spirit."*

*Psalms 34:18*

**Praying for Deliverance and Inner Healing for Wounded Souls**

Minister Janice Sales is a servant of the Lord under the covering of Reverend Joseph Greene.

She is the founder of Janice Sales Ministries, and CEO of the Women's Conference called "Pain for my Purpose," Let's Talk About It & Pray. It is a table talk and open discussion for women. Through her Women's Group called "Mission for God," she serves to strengthen the spiritual connection of Faith, Hope, and Love between sisters across the world. Her goal is to win souls to Christ. Minister Sales is also the founder of "Coats 4 Kids," her desire is to secure a child's warmth through the winter season. She is the founder of Let's Talk About It & Pray; a platform to encourage women to trust God and pray. She has founded Morning Praise Broadcast. She is a serial entrepreneur and has also founded Hope and Glory Television Broadcast and 'Jan's Quick Talk, food for thought.' She also offers "Let's talk about it"- A Women's Brunch, a time for women to gather and celebrate fellowship and friendship. Minister Sales has a passion for seeing souls saved and believers empowered to be who God has called them to be.

She desires for each person to know the greatness of their destiny. Her Kingdom focus is healing and deliverance. Black and brown mothers are often the victims of dysfunctional relationships and deep soul wounds. I long to see manifested inner healing for the children of God. The vision is plain; I desire that the people of God will know His will for their lives. I agree with my heavenly Father to stand in faith, declaring the will of God to be done on the earth and in the lives of his people.

\*\*\*\*\*\*\*\*\*\*\*\*\*\*\*\*\*\*\*\*\*\*\*\*\*\*\*\*\*\*\*\*\*\*\*\*\*\*\*

I believe God and trust him with all my heart. I pray for deliverance and healing for wounded souls. I am focused on standing in the gap and interceding for inner healing. There are so many people in this world in a prison of pain and confusion, feeling like their lives are of no value because they cannot see past their prison doors. My own life experience brought me to the revelation of true freedom from a life of inner brokenness and wounded emotions. I was paralyzed by the fear of being alone and rejected. I gave my personal power to someone who captured my mind and wrecked my emotions. I allowed myself to be defined by someone who did not care for me.

I was pacified by manipulation. I was unable to make sound decisions concerning my life and

emotional health. I was trapped in a toxic marriage. I loved with all my heart, but I was not loved in return. I lived in a fantasy of my own making. Despite the pain and the reality of my emotional abuse, I convinced myself that I was loved. I could not recognize true love; I did not know what true love looked like, nor what it felt like. I desperately wanted to be loved and

accepted. I wanted to be valued. I wanted to be respected. I wanted to be happy. I wanted to be

whole. I was severely bruised and traumatized by betrayal, infidelity, and deception. I was in a toxic relationship and intoxicated by the fantasies of my

own mind. It was the only way I could find

relief. I medicated myself by creating an altered

reality with my illusions. I fooled myself. There

was something missing in my life. I knew that it

was love that I needed, but I did not know where

to find the kind of love that I needed. My self-

deception resulted in depression, condemnation,

shame, guilt, and humiliation. I even contemplated

suicide. I remember being so hurt that I

could not smile. It literally hurt me to smile. My

sadness was deep in the core of my being, and I

felt terrible all the time. I needed deliverance and

relief from the pain of my wounded soul. I needed

real love. Real love does not destroy; it empowers. I was becoming physically ill because there

was no healing for my soulish wounds and emotional brokenness. I had to decide whether I

would survive. I decided that I would live and not die; I had hope and a future. I decided that my children needed me to be my best self. I decided that I deserved better than the cheap knock-off brand of love that I was experiencing. I decided that I would accept nothing less than authentic, real love. When I got in position to receive my deliverance, my deliverer showed up. I had a dream; the presence of the Lord visited me, and from his presence, he released his voice. I heard him say, "Bring a women's conference to Cordele because we have so many hurting women." When I received the instruction, I quickly went into action. God assigned people to come and help me birth the vision. In 2004, I had the first "Pain for my Purpose" women's conference. It was a time of great deliverance. I had been given the key to release....The key was to… "Talk about it." Multitudes of women have been blessed. I had to open my mouth and release my testimony. As others opened themselves up to release their pain, they walked into their victory to experience true deliverance. Every year since 2004, the conference has been growing. We have found that the power of telling our story is a tool for deliverance.

We overcome by the blood of the lamb and the word or our testimony. Now I can genuinely say that my smile is real. We must not forget to pray for those who are still in a prison of depression and low self-esteem. We are praying for deliverance and inner healing for wounded souls. We must create a safe space for releasing this pain and grief. God is calling warrior women who will pray in the spirit for the release of the captive. We must join in faith, praying for deliverance. It is time for freedom from the enemy's tactics, schemes, and manipulations. All things are possible with Christ. We can no longer hide our bruises and brokenness, hoping it will get better.

We must actively seek help and receive it. No longer will we allow ourselves to be paralyzed by the fear of being alone or rejected. The supernatural love of God is amazing. There is healing for wounded souls.

## Prayer for Deliverance and Inner Healing for Wounded Souls

*All praises to the God of heaven and lover of our souls. Your love is amazing. You are our healer. You see all our scars, bruises, and wounds. Nothing is hidden from your sight. You see into our innermost being. You know our every thought. You are concerned about the pain of our broken hearts.*

*You see the deepest wounds of our souls. We are open and transparent in your presence. Heal us from the effects of dysfunctional relationships. Set us free from the prison of our minds. Deliver us from self-deception and altered realities created by our own fantasies. Help us to know the difference between real love and a fake substitute. Teach us to hold ourselves in high esteem because we are made in your image. Teach us to make sound decisions concerning our emotional health. Father, surround us with people who value and respect us. Help us to recognize the tactics, schemes, and manipulations of the enemy.*

*Remove us from the forces that would cause us to be depressed. Separate us from anything or anyone that would cause us to have low self-esteem. Teach us to take the pain of our experience and convert it into the power to*

*achieve our purpose. Remove from us the fear that would silence us. Make us bold and*

*courageous to share our testimony. Show us how to search for the help we need to be happy,*

*healthy, and whole. Let us never be paralyzed by fear of rejection. Grant us to experience your*

*supernatural love. It is your agape love that will heal our wounded souls.*

*Surround us with praying women of war who are not afraid to contend for the release of captives and restoring of sight to the blind. Remove the shame and the guilt of exposing our weakness and bruising. We are calling for the deliverer. Thank you for the opportunity to gain experience in grace. Thank you for opening the door to the prisons of our minds. Thank you for healing our wounded souls. Thank you for healing our spirit man. Thank you for your inner healing. Amen.*

# CHAPTER 3

### *Kristy Chance Starke*

*"Whither shall I go from thy spirit? or whither shall I flee from thy presence? If I ascend into heaven, thou art there: if I make my bed in hell, behold, thou art there. If I take the wings of the morning, and dwell in the uttermost parts of the sea. Even there shall thy hand lead me, and thy right hand shall hold me." (KJV Psalms 139:7-8)*

## Praying for Adult Children

Kristy Chance Starke is a proud servant of Jesus

Christ. She is a leader in her community, the first

Black woman to serve on the City of Kingsland,

GA City Council. She is also a veteran of the

37

United States Army, an entrepreneur, an advocate of small business ownership, business success coach, motivational speaker, and leadership and human resources expert. In 2020 she became a published author of her first book, "Level Up: The Ultimate Guide from Inspiration to Elevation".

Kristy is a proud native of Camden County, GA. She is the daughter of Ms. Malissia Chance and the late Leon, "Bo" Chance of Waverly, Ga. She is the middle child, having one brother and one sister whom she adores dearly. She is the devoted mother of four wonderful children, two extremely smart daughters and two incredibly talented sons. She has a bachelor's degree in business administration from Brenau University as well as a

Master's degree in Business Administration from Liberty University. She is currently pursuing a Doctor of Business Administration with a cognate in Executive Leadership at Liberty University. She has an extensive background in Human Resources Management and Sales Management. Kristy is the owner of The Real Estate Queen, LLC. In addition, she is a certified "Life Coach" and has helped many people find their purpose and move forward in starting or growing their own businesses, including Real Estate Portfolios.

Kristy has found that her purpose in life as an "encourager"- using her gifts and talents to elevate people's self-awareness as well as their spiritual awareness. She is the coordinator of the Godhead Interdenominational Prayer Fellowship, Camden

County Location. She is known for bringing groups of people together, cultivating gifts, and talents for the greater good!

\*\*\*\*\*\*\*\*\*\*\*\*\*\*\*\*\*\*\*\*\*\*\*\*\*\*\*\*\*\*\*\*\*\*\*\*\*\*\*

When I consider how I have prayed for my children over the years, I thank the Lord Jesus, for meeting me in every stage of my journey.

When I was a new mommy expecting my first child, I remember being so afraid. I was afraid for my life and asking my twenty-two-year-old self, what if... what if... what if? I'll never forget an older Caucasian gentleman's wise words spoken to me one day while patiently waiting on his elderly wife in the OB/ GYN's office. He must have noticed my fear; yes, I must have looked very scared as I sat there in the office to make my final visit before they admitted me for the birth of my first baby girl. In his quiet southern Texas voice, he told me, "Don't be afraid, sweetie." He said, "How do you think you got here? The same way your mama and all the other women in the world brought a new life into the world, you will too." He continued, "You were created for this! You will do just fine. Say your prayers, and the Good Lord will do the rest." As I let his words sink in, I immediately felt the weight of fear release me. I was not really a praying person back then. I was miles away from my mother and praying grandmother, with a twenty-one-year-old husband who could not even begin to fathom my terror or pain. I realized I had to pray for myself and this young life that I would be bringing into the world. And that is what I did!

Fast forward 18-20 years later when my oldest children (now there are four of them) began leaving home for college or the military, that same fear crept back in as I thought about having to let go of my young adult children as they left the nest for the world. All kinds of questions, worries, and anxieties gripped my soul. What if… what if… what if? By the time, my third child was leaving the nest; I had begun to truly seek the Lord about how to pray for my adult children. Over the years, if I didn't learn anything

else, I learned that I had to take every matter

to God. From the 2:00 AM fevers of crying babies

to bruises, scars, and the rebellious attitudes

of ornery teenagers, I learned how to bring

EVERYTHING before God.

One morning in prayer, as I was praying for my

nineteen-year-old son, who was getting

into some upsetting circumstances in college, the

Lord gave me a vision of myself when I was

nineteen. He said, "Even though you did not know

me back then like you know me now, didn't

you sense that I was with you?" I replied, "Yes,

You were!" All at once, like a movie-reel fast

forwarding, He began to flood my mind with memories of my life when I was 19 and 20. I remembered those crazy, insane, stupid, and ridiculous choices that I made that surely should have been my ruin! But God kept me through them all. Hallelujah!

Then He reassured me, "I am the same God with your children, as I was with you and

your parents before you. Now release them to me! Trust me to be present in their lives, the

same way I am present in yours!" When God said these words, I was done worrying any longer!

I had already planted seeds of faith in their lives, whether I saw any produce yet.

My parents waited a long time to see fruit in me. In fact, my father had already passed by the time I got to the place of truly hearing God for myself. But I am here, and I hear now! The same way my mother and all the women before me prayed for the safe passage of the birth of their

children and the safe passage of their children into young adulthood, I thank God that he gave

me the wisdom on how to pray for them on my own. No matter what happens, I must trust

him with them! Upon hearing these words, I could rest from the fears, anxieties, and the "what ifs,"

because I knew my children had enough Word in their lives to bring them through just like I did.

For that matter, whatever they were not given, God

is still there with them and will provide them

with whatever they need. He knew I would be their

mom, imperfect, yet He gave enough grace

to make it through. He lent them to me for a time. I

made mistakes- just like my parents and the

ones before them- and so will they as parents. But

praise be to God, we serve a God that loves

us, never fails us, and keeps his word to all of us!

Now they are flying on their own, and I know

my God is with them!

With this, I say to Black and Brown mothers to

trust God! He indeed loves his creation

(mankind) to the ends of the earth- even to hell and back! Our children cannot go anywhere out

of his presence. Believe that!

## Prayer for Adult Children

*Father in the name of Jesus, I bring my adult children before you, and I thank you for their lives. God, thank you for the covenant of protection that you have with believers. You poured out your Spirit upon us and*

*promised that our sons and daughters will prophesy. And I believe that my adult children will find you, hear your voice, and speak the Word of God! God, I thank you that you promised to be present with my adult children wherever they may go. Your word says in Psalms 139:7-8 that you love them so much! You proclaimed there is no place on earth or beyond that they can go without your Spirit present with them. You, Lord, can give them so much more than I can. You can protect them so much better than I can, and you can love them even greater than I can. Therefore, I will not worry, be anxious, or be fearful about their lives because I know you hold them in your hands forever and ever. Amen!*

*I declare: The fruit of my womb belongs to God, and they are blessed of God! (Deut. 28:4) God upholds my children in his right hand- wherever they go, the Spirit of the Lord is with them!*

*(Psalm 139:9) My children are saved and set aside for the work and purposes of God!*

*God knows the plans He has for my adult children- they are thoughts of peace, not evil, and He will give them an expected end.*

*(Jeremiah 29:11) In Jesus' name!*

# CHAPTER 4

## *Patricia I. Woolfolk*

***So, remove grief and anger from your heart and put away pain from your body, because childhood and the prime of life are fleeting Ecclesiastes 11:10***

## Praying for the Mental Wellbeing of Mothers

Patricia I. Woolfolk is the mother of two daughters and nine loving grandchildren. She is a Certified Nursing Assistant and Certified Forklift Driver.

She is the founder of "We build Life Outreach

Ministry." Patricia completed 11 years of High

School before becoming the primary caregiver for

her mother and younger siblings. Patricia's

greatest joy is to follow the pathway of God's

instruction. Dr. Gloria Walton sponsored the

contribution of this co-author.

"Come to Me, all who are weary and heavy-laden,

and I will give you rest. Take My yoke

upon you and learn from Me, for I am gentle and

humble in heart, and you will find rest

for your souls. (Matthew 11:28-30)

*************************************

My name is Patricia I. Woolfolk. I have much to share concerning my experience in life and

concern for the mental well-being of mothers. I have four biological sisters and 3 sisters that do not

share the same mother, no brothers. I grew up in a town called Macon, Georgia. For as long as I

can remember, prayer has always been an essential part of my life. I was raised in a Christian

home. We attended a holiness church. As a child, I could see that my mother and father both

loved the Lord, but something traumatic happened that shook our connection to the church.

The situation influenced every member of the congregation, but it was toughest on my father.

He loved the Lord and held the leaders in high esteem. Infidelity often causes tragic results. The worst part was that my father lost faith in God and went back to his old ways. It was devastating.

It was devastating because my mother held on for dear life to the only thing that gave her identity and comfort. The church, the leaders, the congregation, and my father gave her meaning. It did not matter to her; whatever her husband did, she accepted. We pleaded with my father that he did not have to attend that church; we could at least attend another church. But he was not interested in attending another church.

I was so stressed by the environment, the anger, and the abuse that I sought the easiest way out. I got married at the age of fifteen with my parent's permission. I thought that I had escaped. But the wedge between my parents grew wider until my father finally left. My father had become an angry, abusive womanizer. He drank to excess; he exploited my mother financially, emotionally, even socially, and then he abandoned her.

The stress and the strain of the dysfunction became so intense that my mother had a nervous breakdown and could no longer care for herself or her family. We were advised to institutionalize her. I could not allow that to happen, so I returned to care for my mother.

Mental health services were limited in our community. I knew that I had assumed too much responsibility for a 16-year-old, but I did not feel that I had a choice. At that time, it was the only option I could see. I could not figure out a pathway that would not require me to sacrifice everything I wanted in life so, I offered to help my family. When I returned, I soon discovered that my dad had taken my sisters to his girlfriend's house, and my mother was left alone. I brought my sisters back home to live with us. I had to quit school to take care of my mom and sisters. God provided some help for me. One of the ladies from the housing authority took me under her wings to help me.

She was a compassionate person. She helped me

find some financial assistance for my mother

through social security. She also found a house for

us to live in. I started working part-time

through the CETA program. Eventually, my

mother became so dependent that I could no longer

work because she required all my attention. Later,

my dad wanted to return home, and he agreed

to go to rehab for his alcohol addiction. He

recovered and was stable for about 5 years. My

mother also recovered. Then he relapsed. Later,

when my husband and I were getting a divorce,

my husband and father plotted against me.

One day our family had a big altercation.

My mother was attacked, so I stayed with her to protect her. My father came home drunk and attacked me. He shot me in the back. After a few months, my father abandoned my mother again, and I had to return to provide care for her. My mother died about 6 months later from a broken heart. Mental well-being is an important concern for Black and Brown mothers. We must find a way to care for ourselves while caring for others. We must acknowledge our mental health needs. As Black and brown mothers, we must recognize the importance of addressing our mental health needs.

## Prayer for the Mental Wellbeing of Mothers

*Heavenly Father, sometimes the stress of life can become overwhelming. We need you. For the trauma of disappointment and the pain of abuse, we need you. When our emotions*

*are out of control, and our thoughts are random, we need you. Our families are under attack. Our relationships need repair. When our cherished support systems are ineffective to meet our needs, please send the resources and help required for healing. Mothers are crying at midnight, seeking help when love has drained them of life.*

*Children are ashamed and full of fear because of the secrets in our households. We need you. Fathers are mentally imprisoned for years of*

*social dysfunction. We need your strong arms of protection to keep us safe. Teach us how to*

*have safe boundaries. Teach us how to love ourselves so that we can love others well. Let us not accept abuse as a way of life. We need you. Give us the wisdom to create a safe space for those with vulnerable minds. We pray for strength and support for those who care for loved ones with mental illness. We pray for those whose mental illness has become a way of life. We ask you to challenge their darkness with the light of your love. May we learn to practice your loving presence in a time of crisis and experience the peace that assures us you are always around. Let us find the strength to persevere when life is unfair and unkind. Keep us from the fragmentation of our minds. Raise faithful shepherds with integrity, friends, and loved ones who will know when to love without limit. Teach us to know when limits are the only intervention that will work. Let the light of Christ lead us to grace and forgiveness for ourselves and others. Help us seek out the treatment and help we need to be our best selves. Thank you for your promise to walk with us through the valley of the shadow of death. Take away all fear and unbelief.*

*Heal us from addictions and unproductive coping behaviors. Remove the shame and stigma of mental illness and help us to see the value and beauty of each person. Amen.*

# CHAPTER 5

### *Sis. Sara Gaines*

### Praying for Family and Healing

### *Run now, I pray thee, to meet her, and say unto her, Is it well with thee? Is it well with thy husband? Is it well with the child? And she answered, "It is well" (2Kings 4:26)*

Sis. Sara Gaines is a native of Cordele, GA. She is

an anointed Intercessor and a founding member of

the "Anointed Daughters of Prayer (ADOP)."

ADOP is an intercessory ministry that focuses on praying targeted scriptural prayers over family and community concerns. She is an empowered woman of grace and a successful entrepreneur.

She is the President and CEO of "Precious Memories" where she nurtures and mentors children in the underserved population. She is a Deaconess and Usher in the "Body of Christ" church, serving under the leadership of Bishop Joe L. Ridley. She is a faithful believer in Jesus Christ and a servant of the true and living God. She enjoys serving the body of Christ inside and outside of the four walls of the church.

She is married to her high school sweetheart. They have been together for over 50 years. They have two sons, two daughters, and two grandchildren. Sis. Gaines is a proud representative of Black and Brown mothers who pray.

*****************************************

Trying to find my place and seeking to know my purpose was a primary focus of my life and the subject of many prayers. I discovered that prayers are answered in unusual ways. Now I know that our troubles expose our gift and our purpose. No one wants trouble, but everyone has troubles. I learned early in life that prayer is not only important; it is necessary. It is an effective

way to deal with the troubles and concerns of life. I have encountered many troubles in my life, and I agree that troubles can lead to self-discovery. I discovered a need to pray for family and healing. I

remember the day my prayer life went to another level. It was a normal day; nothing unusual was

expected. I heard a big thump on the floor. I ran to the back of the house. My daughter had

fallen; when I came into the room, she was lying on the floor and unconscious. Immediately, I

could feel the power of the Holy Spirit rising in me to pray. I rebuked the spirit of death; I called on the Lord to rescue my daughter. At that point, the spirit of intercession was activated within me. Tragedy awakened my purpose. My daughter survived. The Lord answered my prayer, and I was ushered into a new normal. My daughter had residual kidney problems. Now, my focus was on healing. Health disparities in the Black and brown populations are well documented. Black and brown mothers are often overwhelmed by the impact of illness and disease affecting the family. From the youngest to the oldest, the probability of disease is vastly increased in the population of black and brown people. This significant factor influenced the prayers of Black and Brown mothers.

It is a part of the unique experience affecting the prayers of the mothers. Black and Brown mothers are often overwhelmed by the impact of disease in the family. I continued to pray for my family and to pray for healing. Later, I noticed that the Holy Spirit began speaking to me in unusual ways. He would highlight certain scriptures in my mind that would prove to be relevant to my next challenge. One day during my meditation, I was drawn to the story of the Shunammite woman in 2Kings, 4th chapter. I was alerted in my spirit that this woman whose son had a stroke and died had unusual faith. After her son died, she laid him in the prophet's bed and declared, "All is well."

She did not panic. She did not fear. She immediately went into action to intervene in the situation. She displayed an amazing level of faith in interceding for her family. She stood in the gap for her son's life and his healing. In the evening on that same day, my husband came home from work. He was not feeling well. He collapsed. The ambulance was called. He had a stroke. But I was able to declare "All is well." He recovered. It was God's grace at work. I accepted my assignment and calling as an intercessor. A few years later, I was drawn to the Prayer of Serenity. "God, grant me the Serenity to accept the things I cannot change. Courage to change the things I can, And Wisdom to know the difference." I was visiting my sister. We were very close. As we sat talking and reminiscing, we made a declaration, "Not even death can separate us." Later that night, I had a

dream that I was walking around in my sister's yard, and I saw two graves. It was a small one

and a large one. I asked a question. "What is this? Where are we going to bury them? I awakened. The dream troubled me. My sister's daughter was pregnant. A few days later, we were eagerly expecting the baby's delivery. She went into labor. The baby died. When they told my sister, she had a heart attack and died also. We were devastated. Prayer warriors, family, and friends surrounded us with love and prayer. This time I was the recipient of the family prayer.

Intercessors need prayer too. I am still declaring "All is well." I am an intercessor called to pray for family and healing.

### Prayer for Family and Healing.

*Father, your love for us is sure. You proved your love by sending your son to die for us. You are our healer. You are our deliverer. You are our great physician. We thank you for the promises that you have made. We know that every promise in Christ is yes and amen. I lift my family to you and ask for your divine protection. Lord, you know every challenge. You see every situation. It is your will that we experience household salvation. I am asking that my family be saved.*

*According to Acts 16:31, it is your will that my whole household is saved. I agree with your will for our salvation. I offer our bloodline and our generations to you for Kingdom purpose. May the righteousness of God take root in our family. Acts 2:39 assures me that this promise is for me and my children, even for generations to come, for all whom the Lord my God will call. I declare that all my children will be taught of the Lord, and great will be their peace (Isaiah 44:3). Father, you are our refuge and strength. You are an ever-present help in times of trouble;*

*therefore, we will not fear. You give us stability and peace when life presents unexpected situations. When it feels like our entire world is shaking and like there is trouble everywhere, you are our peace. (Psalm 46:3). When sickness and disease attack and we walk amid trouble, you preserve our lives. You stretch out your hands against the anger of our enemies. With your right hand, you save us. You are our rock, our fortress, and our deliverer. It is in you that we take refuge. You are our shield and the horn of our salvation. You are our stronghold. (Psalm 18:2) We cast all our cares upon you, and you sustain us. You will never let the righteous fall. (Psalm 55:22) Father, you are our refuge in times of trouble. We are confident that you care for us. (Nahum 1:7) We will wait for you, Lord, and be strong, for we are assured that even though we may have trouble in this world, we can take heart, for you have already overcome the world. (John 16:33) Amen.*

## CHAPTER 6

### *Sheila Surrey*

*"For I know the plans I have for you, declares the LORD, plans to prosper you and not to harm you, plans to give you hope and a future." (Jer. 29:11)*

**Praying to understand God's will for my life**

As children, we have questions about our lives:

why I was born in this family, this state, this

country, etc. We have questions about our parents.

Why do we have the parents we have? Will we have their flaws, (alcoholism, drug addiction, abusive behavior, emotional neglect, etc.)? The list can go on concerning many characteristics and attributes. There is always something we think that our caregivers could have done better or differently. I know that I had these questions because I lost my mother when I was thirteen years old. The situations and circumstances I experienced through my teenage and early adult years were very challenging. The choices and decisions that I thought were best for me were not always the best. Then I would question God about the things I was experiencing.

My parents believed in Jesus and took us to church, so I knew there was a God, but I still questioned him and thought I was bad and not loved by anyone. After my mother passed away, I felt I did not have a voice. I was never asked how I felt and how my mother's passing affected me. I felt like I was just tossed to the side, just like I believed I would be. I went to stay with my sister. My father thought it was best for me. Being a teenager, I began to develop my own way of thinking about how things should be through the eyes of my environment. Unfortunately, before I could really understand what life was truly about, my innocence was taken by an individual close to my family.

Through that experience and others that followed, I developed the mindset that sex showed love. Then I rebelled against the environment I was in with my sister, I ran away with a man and later married him at the age of sixteen, still a child at heart. I thought that I had finally found someone to love me and take care of me. I was never taught what love or even marriage was about. I was still associating love with sex and giving men what I thought they wanted. I was in a mentally abusive relationship and didn't understand why. My husband supplied the material needs; I had a nice home, decorated the way I wanted, and drove a nice car. I was still lonely and felt unloved.

He stayed out all the time and eventually started living with another woman in the same development where we lived. He still took care of me by paying the bills but not giving me any attention. One day, I decided that I would commit suicide; I got some pills, and while getting the drink I was prepared to drink, I started asking God why I was so lonely, why I did not have my mother or father, or anyone to love me? I was just miserable and wanted a way out. But I really didn't want to die; I wanted to be loved. I didn't take the pills and stayed in the marriage until I was 21 years old. I was living in Dallas, Texas at the time and decided to leave and go back home.

After returning home, I was happy to be there with my sister, now thinking that I could make my own decisions for myself and not have to listen to anyone when it came to me. Unfortunately, I did what I wanted to do for the next five years. I still was looking for love, like the song says, in all the wrong places. Then I started questioning God. We all have experienced times where we question and think, "Where is GOD or even if there is a GOD," when issues do not line up with the way we think they should. Then I decided I wanted a baby who would love me unconditionally. Due to the issues of being raped and getting abortions, based on my sister's decisions, I had trouble conceiving. I prayed and asked God to help me; I later had surgery to help me conceive. Life was truly a struggle because I still made the wrong decisions. Even after being blessed with a beautiful daughter, I felt alone and unloved; then, I started using drugs to console my loneliness. That led me on a downward spiral. I lost my job after 18 years; throughout all this, I still went to church. At one service, I went to a lady who had a testimony about being on drugs, and God delivered her without going to rehab. Throughout my time of drug usage, I remembered that testimony. I remember hearing the scripture that says, "God has no respect for persons; what he does for others he will do for you." After getting high and spending all my money, I would pray those words to God. Yes, I lost my job, but God had a better plan. Once I allowed the Lord to truly come into my life, it was still a process for the next ten years. Learning how to have an intimate relationship with the Lord did not stop the problem but helped me get through them with HIS help. Therefore, all the trials and tribulations we experience in life are to help and position us to fulfill the plans and purpose that God has for each one of us. God created all for his purpose and plan, but until we accept Him as our Savior and Lord, we just live our lives to please our fleshly desires. As I continued to read God's word and it helped me. Jeremiah 1:5-6 and 29:11.

Ministry is not just at church; we all are called to impart God's word on our jobs, to our neighbors, in-store lines through basic conversations, telling our personal testimony of what God has done for us and how good He is to us. That is why God's word says, "So let your light shine before men that they may see you and glorify your Father in heaven." First, we need to understand God's position in our lives. God is omniscient (all-knowing). Therefore, we need to understand that God is no stranger to the happenings or situations we experience in our lives. Knowing that God is omnipresent (is everywhere) in everything and every situation we face in our lives. So let us learn through Christ what our responsibility is as we walk in what God has purposed for us. Seek to understand the will of God for your life.

## Prayer to Understand God's will for my life

*Father, the bible says that you knew me before I was formed in my mother's womb, and that you set me apart and appointed me, and that you know the plans you have for me, to prosper me and not to harm me, plans to give me hope and a future. I am perplexed; I've heard your word. I've seen others testify and praise you for your work. I need you to come into my life, allowing me to experience that same love and joy that I see others have with you, knowing that you are God. Father, I come before you first saying, Lord, here I am. I come before you.*

*I acknowledge you as God and my Father, knowing that you hear me even though sometimes I feel alone, scared, and unloved. Your word tells me to cast all my anxieties, worries, and concerns upon you, Lord, because you care about me and my deepest affections. I pray that you would open my heart and mind to be receptive to the guidance of your Holy Spirit, teaching me more of your ways. Not pursuing men's ways, not by traditions or religious mindset but through intimacy with you, Lord. I am coming to you with the spirit of a child not knowing which way to turn or what to do. Help me to understand who I am in You.*

*Your word says, if I confess with my mouth and believe in my heart that Jesus is the son of God, I am saved and that through Jesus I am saved by Your grace. Ephesians 2:8-9 AMP; For it is by grace [God's remarkable compassion and favor drawing you to Christ] that I have been saved [delivered from judgment and given eternal life] through faith. And this [salvation] is not of yourselves [not through your own effort], but it is the [undeserved, gracious] gift of God; not because of [your] works [nor your attempts to keep the Law], so that no one will [be able to] boast or take credit in any way [for his salvation]. Lord, I repent and accept you as my Lord and Savior; help me to become like you. Like the scripture says in Roman 12: 2, "Don't copy the behavior and customs of this world but be a new*

*and different person with a fresh newness in all*

*you do and think. Then you will learn from your*

*own experience how his ways will really satisfy*

*you." (Living Bible). Father, I thank you that you*

*help me to understand your will for my life.*

# CHAPTER 7

### *Sister Barbara Joanne Bivins*

## Praying for the Children

*But Jesus said, "Let the little children come to me and do not hinder them, for to such belongs the kingdom of heaven." (Matthew 19:14)*

Sister Barbara Joanne Bivins is a mother, friend, Sunday school teacher, and mentor. She is a servant of the Most High God and a woman after God's own heart. Sister Bivins represents women whose hopes and dreams have been delayed but not denied. At 76 years of age, she wrote and published her first book because God is faithful to fulfill His promises even to great-great-grandmothers. Her prayer journal is entitled "God is our Help." She has created a legacy of faith and hope in the Word of God for generations to come. Her motto for life is "Ask God, then trust and obey." Sis. Bivins is a prayer warrior and Prophetic Seer. She is the Founder and President of the "Anointed Daughters of Prayer (ADOP)." ADOP is an intercessory ministry that focuses on targeted scriptural prayers for family and community concerns. She journals her prayers and revelations to preserve her authentic and relevant encounters with the Holy Spirit. Her journals are a source of wisdom and enlightenment for a generational legacy of faith and hope.

"See that you do not despise one of these little ones. For I tell you that in heaven their angels always see the face of my Father who is in heaven." (Matthew 18:10)

\*\*\*\*\*\*\*\*\*\*\*\*\*\*\*\*\*\*\*\*\*\*\*\*\*\*\*\*\*\*\*\*\*\*\*\*\*\*\*\*\*

I was young, and now I'm old, but I can say with confidence and assurance that when we cry out to the Father in Jesus' name, He hears us and answers our prayer. When I was young, I had the concerns of a young, black, single mother. I had to make sure that my children were clothed, fed, and had a roof over their heads. Living as a single black mother in America, I experienced my share of

THE PRAYERS OF BLACK AND BROWN MOTHERS

injustice. I was greatly influenced by poverty. No matter how hard I worked, my income was always below the poverty level. I worked as a housekeeper in hotels; I worked as a presser in a cleaner. I cleaned houses, cooked, and cared for the elderly. I earned an honest living. There were times when I wanted my children to participate in extracurricular activities, but we had no money for uniforms or instruments.

There were times when my children missed the opportunity to take a field trip to a faraway place. Our dwelling needed work and maintenance. Our roof sometimes leaked. We did not take summer vacations to exotic places. There was no money for summer camps. Most of the time, my children spent their summers with a neighborhood babysitter. Yes, we lived on the wrong side of the tracks, but God was still good to us. Now I am a great, great grandmother. I can testify that through it all, God was with me. He took care of my family and me. Of all the things I have done for survival and success, the single most important thing was having a prayer life. I was a teenage mother. I learned to pray. I was still developing emotionally, physically, financially, and socially. There was no responsible male figure in our lives. God was our protector and our help. We did not have extended family ties. My mother helped me to raise my children. Our relationship was often strained and complicated, but we prayed. We were not perfect; we had our flaws, but we prayed, and God answered our prayers. With any relationship, communication is the key to success. Prayer is the key to maintaining a relationship with our heavenly Father. I learned that I could talk to him about anything and everything. It is important that we do. That is what I did. I prayed. I trusted God, and he always brought me out. I got involved in some abusive relationships, but he brought me out. I did not die in my process. He brought me out. What can I say about the importance of prayer? It is the most important thing to do. Prayer sets the mind. Prayer calms the spirit. Prayer gives direction. Prayer calls for supernatural help. Prayer releases the light so that the darkness of oppression and depression must flee. Prayer gives strength when we are weak. Prayer is the avenue through which we connect to the resources and wisdom of heaven. I learned to pray that my children's spiritual, emotional, and physical needs would be met.

## Prayer for the Children

*Father, I thank you for allowing me to see the day when I can give voice to the challenges I have experienced and embrace my experience as a black mother. I thank you for allowing me to be a part of this intercessory group of black and brown mothers. Thank you for women of precious faith who identify with kindred challenges and have the testimony of your grace. Thank you for the wisdom of my years. Thank you for the special grace that comes with being a black mother. I come to you and speak from my experience of being the mother of a daughter who was looked over in the school system for special advancement, but you sent an advocate to speak for my child even when I did not know how she was being bypassed because of the color of her skin. I pray that you will provide watching eyes and listening ears to advocate for every child that would be looked over, ignored, or denied because of the color of their skin. I come to you as the mother of a son singled out to be treated unfairly because the application of the law has been structured to hurt him and fragment his purpose on the earth. I declare, "Our help comes from the Lord, the maker of heaven and earth." We pray for the protection of every child, pleading the blood of Jesus over the school grounds, the buses, the classrooms, the bathrooms, and the parking lots. We call for the warring angels to war on behalf of our children. We stand together in faith in Jesus' name. We rebuke the spirit of violence and bullying. We bind the hand of the enemy concerning human trafficking and drug abuse. We lift the parents and ask that every need be met, spirit, soul, and body. In Jesus' name. Amen.*

# CHAPTER 8

### *Evangelist Gloria Harvey Crowder*

*That you be renewed in the spirit of your mind, and put on the new self, which in the likeness of God has been created in righteousness and holiness of the truth (Ephesians 4:23-24)*

## Praying for My Child's Mental Wellness

Evangelist Gloria Harvey Crowder served as the

founder and Senior Pastor of "Church of the

Living God Outreach Ministry Inc" in Macon, GA.

Evangelist Crowder served as a pastoral shepherd for over 18 years. Additionally, she is also the founder and CEO of "Truth and Hope Talk Show" on YouTube. From this platform she has encouraged men and women from diverse backgrounds to embrace the authentic experiences of their lives through 'Truth and Hope', while being empowered to move forward. As a serial entrepreneur, Ms. Crowder is the owner of Glorious Soul Food, a take-out restaurant that she launched right from her back door. She is a woman of courage and creativity. She loves everyone she encounters; her motto is "Anybody can change." She currently enjoys spending time with her close friends and traveling. She delights in loving her family and spending quality time with them. With an infectious smile and a great big heart of love,

Ms. Crowder spreads the joy of the Lord

everywhere she goes.

\*\*\*\*\*\*\*\*\*\*\*\*\*\*\*\*\*\*\*\*\*\*\*\*\*\*\*\*\*\*\*\*\*\*\*\*\*\*\*\*

## Praying for My Child's Mental Wellness

I am the mother of ten children. You can imagine

the joys and sorrows of having such a wonderfully

large family. I had 5 girls and 5 boys. I remember

one summer, after moving back to my hometown

for a year, I transitioned back to Macon, GA.

My son, who had experienced head trauma from a car accident at the age of 15, was now 19 and started experiencing delusions. He was talking to himself and fighting in the air. He cut off half of his hair. He was demonstrating bizarre behavior. It was a frightening experience. We accessed mental health assistance. It was his first episode. We all felt so helpless. It was a tough time for the whole family. I went into a severe depression and cried continuously. I felt as if I had lost my son. We never expected this to happen to him. We were all so proud of him. He was well-liked by everyone. He had shown such a promising future. He was the mascot of his school.

He was brilliant and got good grades. This changed everything and it drove me to my knees. He was diagnosed with Schizophrenia and Bipolar Disorder. He became overly aggressive. He was unpredictable. Once while I was driving, he attacked me. He was sitting behind me and snatched me by the hair, hitting me in the head. I almost had an accident. It was a traumatic experience. I loved my son, but I was afraid of him. On another occasion, he attacked me again. It caused an altercation that ripped through the family, creating divisions that were difficult to heal. My heart was broken because I love all my children. He was so delusional that he no longer recognized me as his mother.

He disowned me for about 10 years. We were estranged. There was so much anger and unforgiveness. Whenever I tried to reach out to him, he would curse me and call me bad names. It hurt me so much; it wounded me to my soul. I had to pray. It was a long and arduous journey. I begged God to help me get through this. I did not want to hate my child. I did not want him to hate me. I wanted to have a healthy relationship with my son. It was so painful. I was unable to hug him. He could not embrace me. It was a lonely experience. It was emotionally exhausting. My son eventually ended up in a prison near me. One day, I cried out to God; I fell on my knees. I cried from the depth of my heart. I took a picture of my son and placed it on my heart.

I pleaded with God to help me. I talked to the Lord with sincerity. I was as transparent as I could be. I told the Lord honestly how I was feeling. I told him what I wanted. I wanted to put my arms around my son again. I wanted him to call me mama again. I prayed. I stayed on my knees crying out to God until I experienced a breakthrough. I knew within myself that God had answered my prayer. I prayed that God would give my son a sound mind. I knew that God had answered my prayer. Over the next two days, I called the prison to see if I could visit him, but he had to agree to see me. He did agree to see me. It was an answer to prayer, but I didn't know what to expect. When we met, he embraced me and said, "Hey, mama."

God did it! Prayer changes things. The visit went very well. When it was time for me to leave, my son told me that he loved me. I had my son back. The joy that I felt was unspeakable. My eyes filled with tears of joy. I praised the Lord all the way home. I am still praising him and thanking him for answering my prayer. My son still has some challenges, but I am so grateful to God that he answered my prayer. The challenges of having a loved one who needs mental care can often get complicated and painful. Many mothers are praying for their children because they are not mentally or emotionally well. This is a challenge that affects the whole family.

## Praying for My Child's Mental Wellness

*Father in Jesus' name, I come to you presenting my son who is dealing with mental health issues. Father, you know that he can be aggressive and dangerous when he is in a state of confusion. Lord, I need your help. I need you to intervene. My son needs your help. Please restore his mind and give him a sound mind. I ask for your mercy. Lord, I confess, at times, I have been weary. Keep my heart free from resentment and bitterness. Set me free from tormenting memories of the past. There have been times when I just wanted to give up on having a healthy relationship with my son because of his sickness and how he has treated me. But I do not want to give up on my child. You did not give up on me. Your word says, "Blessed are the merciful for they shall receive mercy" (Matt. 5:7). Your word says that if I don't forgive others, then you cannot forgive me. (Matt.6:15) With love and kindness, you draw us unto yourself. Help me to be more like you. I want to be kind, tenderhearted, and forgiving. (Eph. 4:32) Use me so that I can be an instrument of your love. Help me to give unconditional love. Father, please take away all fear and torment from my son. Shield me from all fear and torment. Close every unholy opening in his mind to darkness. Help him resist every thought contrary to your will and destiny for his life. Give my son clarity of thought. Give him clarity of vision.*

*Help him to hear and recognize your voice. Lead him in paths of righteousness for your name's sake. May your perfect will be done in his life. It is your will that my son be healed. You watch over your word to perform it. I declare that whom the Son sets free is free indeed. I agree with the word that my son is set free. May the eyes of his understanding be enlightened. Let him trust in your redeeming quality and experience the peace of salvation. "For God hath not given us the spirit of fear: but of power, and of love, and a sound mind." (II Timothy 1:7). Amen.*

# CHAPTER 9

*Dr. Barbara Whitehead*

**"Before I formed you in the womb, I knew you; before you were born, I set you apart.**

**(Jer.1:5)**

**Praying for the protection and**

**dedication of the Unborn baby**

Dr. Barbara Whitehead is a servant of the Lord.

She is the Founder of "Barbara Whitehead

Ministries," and Senior Pastor of "International

Family of Faith Church."

She is the Founder and CEO of "Confident Kids Inc.," a nonprofit youth organization. She is a well-known radio and television personality. Dr. Whitehead is the CEO and founder of "Kingdom international TV," a global television network providing partnering ministries with the opportunity to take the gospel to the entire world. As CEO and founder of "Health for the Whole Man Ministries," she publishes a bimonthly magazine called "Start Healthy" Dr. Whitehead also produces a weekly national Believers Empowerment Training session, encouraging all believers to walk in their divine kingdom purpose.

She is the founder and co-host of the "Coffee and

Tea Talk Show," discussing real and relevant

issues in the lives of all believers. She is also

CEO/Owner of "3D Destiny Coaching

Services." Dr. Whitehead most treasured and

valued role is to be a friend of God.

\*\*\*\*\*\*\*\*\*\*\*\*\*\*\*\*\*\*\*\*\*\*\*\*\*\*\*\*\*\*\*\*\*\*\*\*\*\*\*\*


Once my mother told me a story that both

intrigued me and challenged me. She told me how

she was advised to abort me because she was a

teenage mother. She told me about how

difficult it was to be pregnant at her age and the

challenges she faced.

I am intrigued that she decided to face the humongous obstacles in her life because she valued my life. She persevered through every situation to give me a chance at life. She became pregnant at the age of fourteen and delivered me at the age of fifteen. She was in distress most of the time and felt isolated and rejected. She was physically and emotionally abused. She longed to feel loved and accepted. There was one thing that she loved to do. She loved to learn new things. One of the most devastating things that she suffered was being put out of school with no alternative for education.

She could not finish her education because she was making room for me, but she was strong, and she refused to give in to the pressure of negative forces that were always attacking. I understand myself better now. I am challenged to be my best self and not accept limits even when it seems that the odds are against me. I am intrigued that her emotional

health and strength could impact my emotional development. She admits that she often prayed for me while carrying me in her womb and dedicated my life to the Lord. She shared how that prayer always seemed to take her to a place of assurance and peace. I believe I heard her praying. Studies have shown that babies can hear in the womb.

Hearing is one of

the first senses that a baby develops in the womb.

The baby's ears develop about the fifth

month of pregnancy. The first sounds that it

detects are the sounds of the mother's body. The

baby hears the mother's heartbeat and breathing.

The baby hears the rush of blood through the

umbilical cord and the mother's gurgling tummy.

One of the most important sounds to a baby is

the sound of its mother's voice.

But it is also sensitive to the mother's emotions.

Many pediatricians say that the mother's

emotional health plays a role in shaping the baby's

emotional development. The American

Academy of Audiology stated that by 25 to 29 weeks, the baby can hear sounds from outside the mother's womb. The baby's emotional development also begins about the sixth month of pregnancy. During this stage of pregnancy, a baby also starts moving. Several studies have shown that babies who are read, played music, sung, or spoken to regularly are often calmer and have a better emotional connection with their parents or caregivers. What a unique and powerful position for a mother; she can purposefully and intentionally help to shape the emotional development of her unborn infant. This is also a dangerous power if it is not used properly. Power is dangerous when it is not understood. This means that exposure to harmful,

negative words and feelings can have a negative impact on the emotional development of an

infant. Emotional development and social development are intricately linked. Social development is what happens when the baby learns to respond to faces and voices. It also means how the child learns to get along with others. This information confirms that the emotional health of the mother will have an impact on the emotional and social development of the baby. With this

understanding, we can see that mothers have both authority and power to impact the future of their unborn babies. A mother's prayer for her unborn infant is effective. It works. Black and brown mothers face a unique set of challenges in life, and so do their children. We must take every opportunity to give our children a strong foundation for a bright future. Each child has a destiny to fulfill. Mothers can pray with confidence for their children's success and dedicate them to the purpose of God's kingdom before the child is born. Mothers can activate favor, protection, and direction for the child's life. Mothers can pray for the future, purpose of their baby, and expect God to hear and answer.

Prayer of Protection and Dedication for the Unborn baby.

Heavenly father, you are a good father who loves his children, and I thank you. You have a plan

and a future for my baby's life. You have declared good thoughts toward my baby and assigned

your expected outcome and destiny (Jer.29:11). I thank you. Before being formed in the womb,

you knew this child and set him/her apart for kingdom destiny. You saw this baby in the womb

before their bodies were formed. You planned out the days of their lives and have written them

in a book. You ordained and approved each day before it came into being (Psalm 139:16). I

thank you. I thank you for access to divine wisdom to parent this child according to their need, foreordained destiny, and purpose (James 1:5).

Father, you have declared that children are a treasure, a heritage from the Lord (Psalm 127:3). I thank you for this treasure, a gift from you. Let this child always know that he/she is a gift and will understand their value. Let this child understand that they are made in the image of the creator and have inherent worth. Let him/her be surrounded by supportive, encouraging family and friends. Help me to teach them that their body is the temple of the Holy Spirit and should be honored as a temple. (I Cor. 6:19-20). Let this child walk in divine health all the days of their life. Shield and protect this child from

every disease and disorder that would damage

their temple. Help me to teach principles of health

and healing that will honor the sacredness of

the body as a temple. Father, please cover this

child with faith and favor all the days of their life.

Thank you that your love has no limit. Thank you

that regardless of the circumstances surrounding

this child's entry into this dimension of time and

space, you love them with an everlasting love.

May they always feel your love and know that they

are accepted.

Let them always have a strong consciousness and

honor for their own unique gifting, while having a

heart of celebration and thankfulness for the

gifting of others. Amen.

Made in United States
Orlando, FL
18 August 2023